TRAVELLING
WILD

JOURNEY
ALONG THE
AMAZON

WAYLAND
www.waylandbooks.co.uk

D0525820

Published in paperback in 2014 by Wayland
Copyright © Wayland 2014

Wayland
Hachette Children's Books
338 Euston Road
London NW1 3BR

Wayland Australia
Level 17/207 Kent Street
Sydney NSW 2000

Commissioning editor: Debbie Foy
Designer: Lisa Peacock
Consultant: Michael Scott
Proofreader/indexer: Susie Brooks
Map illustrator: Tim Hutchinson

A catalogue for this title is available
from the British Library
918.1'1'04

10 9 8 7 6 5 4 3 2 1

ISBN: 978 0 7502 8305 2

Printed in China

Wayland is a division of Hachette Children's Books,
an Hachette UK Company.
www.hachette.co.uk

CONTENTS

The Amazon River   04

The Upper Amazon   06

Indigenous Peoples   08

How the Amazon River is Used   10

The Amazon Rainforest   12

Amazon Fish   14

Reptiles and Amphibians   16

The River in Flood   18

Mammals   20

The Meeting of the Waters   22

The Lower Amazon   24

The Amazon Estuary   26

Journey's End   28

Glossary   30

Index & Further Information   32

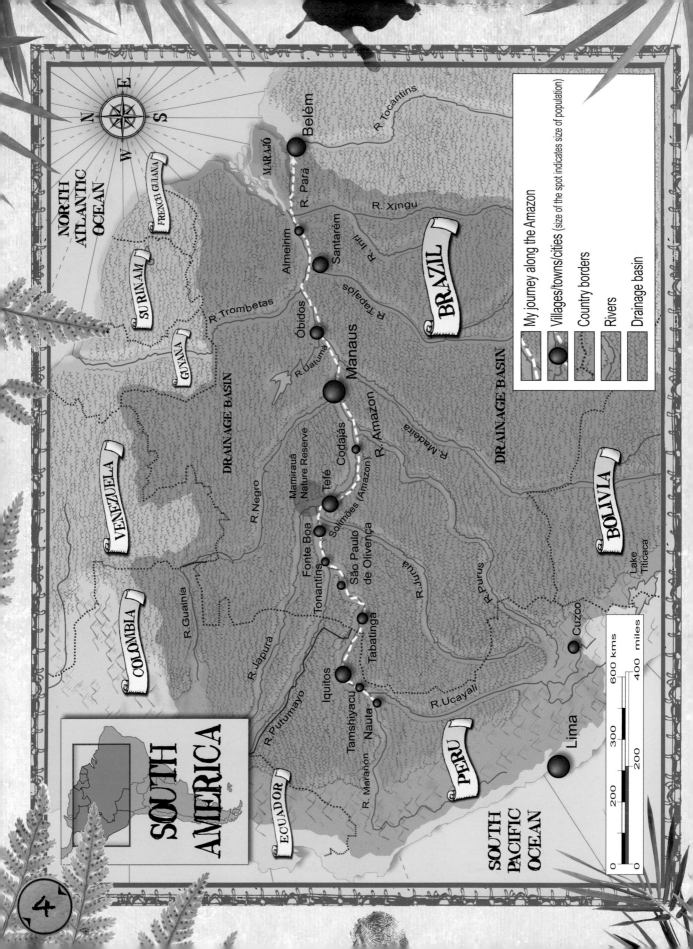

THE AMAZON RIVER

Preparing for the trip

I can't believe I'm actually doing this. On 14 January, I'm going to start my epic journey (see map opposite), paddling the entire length of the Amazon River in a kayak! Six weeks on my own, facing piranhas, caimans, blood-sucking mosquitoes – and who knows what else. I'm nervous, but also excited. I've been training for weeks, and now I just can't wait to get started!

The great river

At 6,400 km long, the Amazon River in South America is the second-longest river in the world, but the biggest in volume of water that flows along it. The outflow from the Amazon contributes about 15% of all the freshwater that enters all of the oceans of the world. It is also one of the world's widest rivers, in places stretching 10 km across, even when it is not in flood.

Climate

The Amazon River is in the tropics, where it's hot and wet throughout the year, with an annual average temperature of 27°C. There's no summer and winter, and temperatures vary by just 2°C throughout the year. There's also no dry season either – it rains all year, although rainfall is typically heaviest between November and March.

Equipment

I've decided to bring the following:
- kayak
- first aid kit (including anti-malarial pills)
- water purification tablets
- map and compass
- box of matches
- string
- pocket knife
- machete
- sun cream
- insect repellent
- sun hat with insect net
- signalling mirror
- tarpaulin (to protect my kit when it rains)
- pot for boiling water
- whistle
- torch

Day 1, 14 January
Nauta to Tamshiyacu

Well, here I am at the start of my journey. After arriving in Lima, the capital of Peru, I flew to Iquitos, and then drove south to Nauta (see map on page 4). This bustling little town is on the Marañón River, close to where it meets the Ucayali River. Why did I choose to start here? Because where these two rivers meet is where the Amazon River begins – or at least that's where it starts being called the Amazon River!

Origins of the river

The river that will eventually become the Amazon actually begins as a small stream called the Huarco, high in the Andes Mountains of southern Peru. From there it flows north, then east, changing its name to Toro, Santiago, Ene, Tambo, Apurímac, Ucayali, and finally Amazon.

Falls and rapids

For much of its early stages, the river runs through narrow gorges. As it descends towards the lowlands, the current flows faster, picking up loose rocks, soil and branches and carrying these downstream. These materials wear away the bed, making the river deeper. Its course is regularly interrupted by falls and rapids, making it very difficult to navigate.

The Urubamba, another source of the Amazon, winds its way through mountain passes in Peru.

Be smart, survive!

I make a shelter each night in the dense rainforest by the river's edge. First, I find two trees about 2 metres apart. I locate a 2-m long log and secure it horizontally between the two trees with vines. Next I attach four or five 3-m long branches, to either side of the horizontal support, to form a tent-like shelter.

Edible vs inedible?

GET OUT ALIVE!!

I gather any edible plants, nuts, roots or berries I can find growing near my shelter. Many plants can be eaten, but some are poisonous. Only a highly experienced traveller should attempt this kind of foraging. If you haven't travelled wild before, the basic rule is: don't eat what you're not sure of.

River meanders

By the time I join the river, it's become very deep and wide. The current is still strong, but because the land is flat the river is full of bends which slows me down. The bends are called meanders and are caused by the fast-flowing river wearing away the outside of the bends and dropping silt on the inside.

INDIGENOUS PEOPLES

Day 1, 14 January
Tamshiyacu to Iquitos

This afternoon, I arrived in Iquitos, a busy, cosmopolitan city in the heart of the Peruvian rainforest. From here, I paddled for an hour up the Momon River, a tributary of the Amazon, to visit some of the indigenous peoples of the area. I could hear the thum-dum, thum-dum of the great manguaré drums of the Bora people, long before I arrived at their riverside village of San Andrés.

Children paddle in front of their house made of babassu straw.

The Bora people

The Bora tribe are divided into clans. They paint their faces with different designs, depending on their clan. They make their clothing using fibres from the inner bark of palm trees, which they colour with natural dyes. The Bora people maintain their customs, including their festivals when they perform traditional dances. The rhythm is provided by beating the ground with long wooden batons, sometimes with shells attached.

The Yagua people

A little further upriver, I encounter a Yagua village. The Yagua people live a simple life of small-scale farming, fishing and hunting. They're talented craftspeople, who make beautiful jewellery out of natural materials like seeds, fibres and animal bones. The men carve animal figures from wood, and make decorative blowguns, called punaca. They blow a poison-tipped dart through the blowgun to hunt birds, monkeys and other small creatures.

Be smart, survive!

To survive, I have to eat. I can't make a blowgun like the Yagua people, but I can make a bow and arrow. First, I find a dry, hardwood stick about a metre long and whittle down the thicker end, so it's an even width. I cut notches at either end of the bow to attach the bow string, which can be any fibrous material such as tree vine. Arrows should be made from straight, dry sticks. I sharpen the tip with my knife and add feathers to the end of the arrow (fletching) to improve its flight.

Snake danger

There are several poisonous snakes in the Amazon rainforest, including the bushmaster and the himeralli. To avoid getting bitten:

GET OUT ALIVE!!

1. Watch your step. Step onto logs rather than over them.

2. Don't harass or corner a snake. Some, like the bushmaster, will attack if cornered.

3. Use sticks to turn logs and rocks.

4. Check bedding, shelter and clothing before you get into it!

HOW THE AMAZON RIVER IS USED

Days 2-6, 15-19 January
Iquitos to Tabatinga

I've spent the past few days paddling through the Peruvian rainforest towards Brazil. After Iquitos, the river became wide and deep, and there have been more fishing boats, kayaks, small cruise ships and cargo vessels. Occasionally, I've passed a native village and seen the people fishing, bathing and doing their laundry. It's made me think of all the many uses humans make of the river.

Commercial waterway

The Amazon rainforest is harvested for its tropical hardwoods, such as teak, purpleheart and mahogany. It is also rich in minerals such as gold, bauxite, iron, tin and diamonds. The river provides a crucial highway for the transportation of these materials to the wider world.

Isolated city

Iquitos is the largest city in the world that cannot be reached by road. The only way to get there is by aeroplane or boat. With a population of 430,000, it depends on the river for trade, transport and communication. Established by the Spanish in the 1750s, Iquitos grew wealthy during the rubber boom of 1890–1914, when it attracted thousands of immigrants from around the world. Today, Iquitos is a centre of the lumber trade, as well as tourism, with around 150,000 visitors per year.

The Amazon River is a major destination for tourists. The more adventurous tourists can be seen wildlife-spotting in a skiff, or paddling kayaks like me. For those who prefer a more comfortable kind of holiday, there are luxury cruises on riverboats, with observation decks and air-conditioned suites.

Fishing

The indigenous peoples of the Amazon depend on fish as a source of protein. Since the 1970s, several commercial fisheries have opened up in the Amazon. Many of the fish they catch end up in aquariums. They use large, motorised fishing vessels and sophisticated equipment to maximise their catch. As a result, local fishermen have reported smaller catches.

Be smart, survive!

Each night, I make a fire. This isn't for warmth as nights are a mild 20–25°C, but for cooking and to deter wild animals. I gather pieces of wood and stack them in a cone shape. Then I place leaves and dry grass inside the cone for kindling. I use matches, kept in a waterproof container, to light the fire.

THE AMAZON RAINFOREST

The rainforest ecosystem

The Amazon rainforest contains more than 40,000 plant species, more than 420 different types of mammal and 1,300 bird species. The trees provide shelter and a habitat for the animals, birds and other plants. All of these organisms interact with and depend on each other in a giant ecosystem.

Days 7-9, 20-22 January
Tabatinga to São Paulo de Olivença

I've now entered Brazil, and the Amazon River has changed its name to the Solimões. The riverbank is a vast, endless rainforest, teeming with animal life. The trills and squawks of birds and screeches of monkeys echo through the air. I've seen the vivid colours of a scarlet macaw flashing by my kayak, and giant trees rising 40 m into the sky. And then for long hours I've seen and heard nothing but rain pounding down around me.

Five layers

There are five layers to this ecosystem. The top two layers form the forest canopy. Monkeys, birds, bats, insects and many other animals are found here. The canopy is like a thick covering that shades the third layer — the shorter trees. The fourth layer is made up of shade-loving shrubs, and the fifth, of ground-level plants. Insects and a few large mammals are found in these lower layers.

Capuchin monkeys live in the rainforest canopy.

Be smart, survive!

A harpoon is a useful weapon to have while camping in the rainforest. You can use it to hunt boar or fish, and also to defend yourself against big beasts like panthers who might decide to hunt you! Find a strong branch that's light enough to throw. Tie your hunting knife or machete to it using rope, shoelaces or vines. Your harpoon is ready for action!

Threats

The Amazon rainforest ecosystem is huge and diverse, yet fragile. The main threat to it is deforestation. Since 1970, almost 745,000 km² (18%) of the Brazilian rainforest have been cleared by loggers and farmers. Rainforest soils are poor in nutrients. Most of the nutrients are found in the above –ground plant growth. This makes recovery difficult.

A mosquito net hat is useful when trekking through the rainforest.

Bloodsuckers

Insect bites can lead to infection – and when you're deep in the rainforest, miles from the nearest hospital, that can mean death. If you've run out of insect repellent, don't worry. Just rub yourself with garlic! It's not just for keeping vampires at bay. Insects also hate it – especially mosquitoes.

AMAZON FISH

Days 10–12, 23–25 January
São Paulo de Olivença to Tonantins

Amazing! I've just seen something quite incredible. A shoal of young arapaima just swam right under my kayak. The arapaima is the largest fish in the Amazon and can be over 2 m long. Experts say it's one of the most ancient fish on Earth, dating from the Jurassic Period. And it's pretty weird for a fish, as it's air-breathing. It's also carnivorous, but luckily it seems to prefer fish to kayakers!

Electric eel

The Amazon has an amazing diversity of river fish. Some experts reckon it's home to up to 5,000 species. The electric eel is one species I hope I never encounter. This fish can grow to around 3 m long and can deliver a 650-volt electric shock, which is enough to stun a man. Believe it or not, it can deliver these shocks up to eight hours after its own death!

How to avoid a piranha attack

1. Piranhas are usually only dangerous when starving. This can happen between April and September when water levels are low, so avoid swimming in these months.

2. Swim at night. Piranhas hunt during the day and sleep at night.

3. Piranhas sense blood and it makes them more likely to attack, so don't swim with an open wound.

~~Candiru catfish~~

This is one of the most feared of all the Amazon river fish – not because of its size (it's only 15 cm long) but because of its method of attack. The candiru is a parasite that enters a larger fish by swimming up an orifice (or sometimes it bites its way inside) and then feeds on its host's blood and organs, becoming increasingly swollen. Basically, it eats its victims from the inside!

I passed by this fisherman who had caught a large arapaima!

Be smart, survive!

Make a simple fishing rod using a long stick, a piece of vine and a hook. Make a hook carved from twigs or bark, or use a metal object, such as a pin, needle or wire. Tie a 2-m long vine (your fishing line) to one end of the stick and attach a small pebble about 10 cm from the bottom of the line for a weight. Attach the hook to the bottom of the line, place some bait on the hook, and start fishing!

REPTILES AND AMPHIBIANS

Days 13–15, 26–28 January
Tonantins to Fonte Boa

The Amazon can be dangerous! Last Wednesday, I was swimming in the shallows, and put my foot down on what I thought was a log. It turned out to be a 4-m long caiman! I jumped, just as it snapped its jaws. It missed me by millimetres! The next day, in a swampy area near the bank, I came across a giant yellow anaconda. Luckily, it was too busy feasting on a wild pig to even notice me!

Mamirauá Nature Reserve
Fonte Boa
Tonantins
Tefé
Solimões (Amazon)
Codajás
São Paulo de Olivença
Tabatinga
R. Amaz

The caiman

Caimans live in the wetlands of Central and South America and are close relatives of the alligator. There are five species of caiman. The largest of these, the black caiman, can reach nearly 6 m in length. These predators hunt at night, snapping mammals, birds and fish in their powerful jaws.

Be smart, survive!

Rainforest animals such as geckos and jaguars use camouflage to avoid detection. We can also use it to help us hunt! Animals will run from a human shape, so break up your outline by attaching small amounts of vegetation to your clothes and hat. Use mud or charcoal from burned wood to cover exposed skin.

Poison dart frog

This extraordinary amphibian secretes poison through its skin. It got its name because rainforest dwellers traditionally used this poison on the tips of their blow darts. The most toxic of all poison dart frogs is the golden poison frog, which has enough poison to kill between 10 and 20 humans.

Anaconda

One of the largest and heaviest snakes in the world, the anaconda lives in the swamps and rivers of tropical South America. It feeds on fish, birds, caimans and mammals. The anaconda kills its prey by coiling around it and crushing it to death, then swallows its victims whole. It has a flexible jaw that allows it to swallow large animals.

Coral snake danger

GET OUT ALIVE !!

The highly venomous coral snake is one of the most dangerous snakes in the Amazon, so it's best to know what it looks like in case you come across one. About 60 cm in length, it's covered in rings of black, red and yellow. There are some non-venomous snakes with similar colouring, but the only safe rule is to avoid them all!

THE RIVER IN FLOOD

Days 16–19, 29 Jan –1 Feb
Fonte Boa to Tefé

It's the fourth week of my journey and days and weeks have lost all their significance. It's now early February, which is the middle of the wet season here in the Amazon. The river is in flood, and you can barely tell where the river ends and the forest begins. It's a great time to be a river predator, as your hunting grounds expand enormously!

The flood season

From December to June, high rainfall and snow-melt in the Andes Mountains to the west make the river level rise dramatically. It can rise by up to 15 m and floods an area the size of England. It swells from around 6–8 km at its widest to nearly 40 km, almost tripling the land area it covers!

Várzeas and igapós

Seasonally flooded forests in the Amazon Basin are known as várzeas or igapós. Várzeas are flooded by 'whitewater' rivers, such as the Solimões and the Madeira, rich in mountain silt. An igapó is a forest flooded by a 'blackwater' river, such as the Negro or Tapajós. These rivers have flowed through swamplands where decaying vegetation has stained their waters black.

Brazilian wandering spider

One of the world's deadliest arachnids, the Brazilian wandering spider has a bite venomous enough to kill a human. It gets its name because of its habit of wandering about in search of prey, and is often found in cosy, dark places like shoes or clothing. So remember to take extra care when dressing each morning!

Creatures of the flooded forest

Every year during the flood season, fish, reptiles and other water creatures migrate into the várzeas and igapós to feed and reproduce. For example, the hunting grounds of the caimans expand enormously in this season. When the floodwaters recede, the creatures return to the main river.

Tambaqui

The trees of the flooded forest rely on these seasonal visitors to disperse their seeds. Fruit-eating fish like the tambaqui eat the seeds that fall from the trees. The seeds pass through their bodies and are then excreted to sprout somewhere else.

Be smart, survive!

The tambaqui is a tasty fish, and easy to catch if you know how. The fish waits beneath the rubber tree to catch its seeds. If you stand next to a rubber tree and imitate the falling seeds using a long branch with a seed attached by a line, you'll soon lure a tambaqui to the surface where you can harpoon it.

MAMMALS

Days 20-24, 2-6 February
Tefé to Codajás

This has to be the highlight of my trip so far, I've just been swimming with boto - or pink river dolphins! I was taking a dip in the dark, clear waters of an igapó when I saw bubbles rising to the surface. Suddenly two boto came past me! One swam close and I couldn't resist reaching out and touching it as it glided by. I also saw a giant otter eating a fish. What an amazing day!

Pink river dolphin

These beautiful creatures spend the rainy season feeding on fish in the igapós. They navigate their way through the flooded forest, helped by a highly flexible neck that allows them to manoeuvre around sunken trees. Their snouts help them to extract fish hiding in hollow logs and submerged plants.

Signalling mirrors

I've packed a small signalling mirror in case the worst happens and I need to be rescued. If you hold a mirror up to the sun and wobble it around, it catches the sunlight and sends out a bright flash that can be seen up to 60 km away on a clear day. Hopefully, I could use this to attract the attention of a search and rescue helicopter.

Mamirauá

Near the town of Tefé, where the Japura River joins the Solimões, I come across a nature reserve called the Mamirauá. During the rainy season, the Mamirauá becomes the largest flooded forest reserve in Brazil. Among the protected species to be found here is the Amazonian manatee. This unusual-looking creature has a hairless, seal-like body, a flattened rear end, paddle-like forelimbs and hippo-like snouts! They can grow to 3 m in length.

THE MEETING OF THE WATERS

Days 25-28, 7-10 February
Codajás to Manaus

I've reached Manaus, the biggest city of the Amazon basin. With nearly two million inhabitants, it's quite a culture shock for me, having been on my own for so long. Manaus is located at the meeting point of the Negro and the Solimões Rivers. It's quite a sight seeing the black waters of the Negro and the silt-rich white waters of the Solimões flowing alongside each other before gradually mixing. From here on, all the way to the Atlantic, the river is called the Amazon.

The rubber boom?

During the 19th century, South America was the world's main source of rubber. The latex sap from rubber trees was harvested and sent along the Amazon River to the coast, and onwards to Europe. As a major river port, Manaus grew wealthy from the rubber trade. Rubber barons built fine villas and a grand opera house. But in 1876, a British trader smuggled rubber seeds out of the Amazon. By the early 1900s, rival plantations had been set up in South—East Asia. The rubber boom was over and Manaus fell into poverty.

Manaus today

Today, Manaus has become wealthy again. It is no longer reliant on one product, but a variety of industries including timber, Brazil nuts, brewing, shipbuilding, soap manufacture, petroleum refining, chemical manufacture and tourism. It is the largest city in northern Brazil, covering over 11,000 km^2 and with a population of 1.86 million.

Farming the floodplain

This part of the river is surrounded by a low, flat floodplain called the várzea. In the wet season it's flooded by white waters rich in fertile silt, which makes it ideal for farming. The farmers live in houses on stilts to avoid the floods and live by catching fish. When the floods recede they plant their crops in the fertile soil, growing beans, corn, watermelon and manioc.

Caboclos

The Caboclos are a people of the várzea. Some are Amerindians (indigenous), while others are mestizo (of mixed indigenous and European descent). During the 18th century, the Caboclos were hired by the Portuguese rulers of Brazil as 'rubber soldiers' — sent into the Amazonian interior to harvest rubber. Today, they fish, hunt in the forest and farm. They build their houses on stilts or floating tree-trunk rafts.

Poisonous manioc!

Farmers turn manioc tubers (roots) into a flour called farinha, used to make bread. But manioc tubers are highly toxic, and if not properly prepared they can cause severe illness or even death. To make the manioc tuber safe, farmers soak it for 18–24 hours. They then grind it into flour, soak it in water again, then squeeze it dry several times and toast it.

GET OUT ALIVE!!

THE LOWER AMAZON

Days 29-34, 11-16 February
Manaus to Óbidos

After leaving Manaus, I've paddled east through a vast floodplain. The river is muddy brown from the silt, and as wide as an inland sea. After the teeming life of the rainforest there's little to look at, apart from sunken trees, houses on stilts and the occasional tourist riverboat. At the city of Santarém, the Tapajós River, with its relatively clear, silt-free waters, joins the Amazon. I spent a relaxing afternoon there on one of its beautiful freshwater beaches.

The changing river

During the wet season, the Lower Amazon floods vast areas of land. In the dry season, the river shrinks to its main channel, which winds through the floodplain. At the city of Óbidos, the Amazon becomes much narrower, deeper and faster, as the land forms itself into a natural channel between two mountain ranges. The Portuguese, who ruled Brazil from 1500 to 1815, built a fort at Óbidos in 1697. The Amazon is just 2 km wide here – narrow enough for the Portuguese to see the far side and keep watch for enemies.

Avoid getting attacked by a bull shark

1. Stay out of the water at dawn, dusk or at night, when they're most likely to feed.
2. Don't enter the water if you have an open wound. Bull sharks can detect even tiny amounts of blood.
3. Don't wear high-contrast clothing or shiny jewellery. Sharks are attracted by these things.
4. Don't splash around too much. Swim with steady, rhythmic strokes.
5. If turtles and dolphins start to behave erratically, leave the water.

GET OUT ALIVE !!

Tides and what they bring

Ocean tides reach as far as 800 km up the river, allowing marine wildlife like bull sharks to drift upstream. Bull sharks have been known to attack people in rivers and estuaries. Other creatures, like stingrays, have adapted to live in fresh water and now thrive in the river.

Stingrays can deliver very painful stings, though these are rarely fatal to humans.

THE AMAZON ESTUARY

Map showing route from Óbidos to Almeirim, with locations including Manaus, Óbidos, Almeirim, Santarém, R. Pará, R. Uatumã.

Days 35-39, 17-21 February
Óbidos to Almeirim

I'm now in the Amazon estuary, and on the final leg of my journey. I'm looking forward to a hot shower and clean clothes, though I'm sad that this amazing experience is nearing its end. But the excitement isn't over yet. In fact, one of the most nerve-shredding moments of the entire trip happened yesterday when I saw a tidal bore (a 4-m high wave) roaring upriver towards me. I was capsized by it, but luckily I, and my equipment, survived the ordeal!

River islands

The Amazon's estuary is more than 300 km long and filled with lots of low-lying forested islands. Because the river discharges so much water into the Atlantic (see page 5), very little salt water gets into the estuary. Despite this, the estuary is highly affected by tides, which flood most of its islands twice a day.

Tidal bores

The Amazon sometimes experiences tidal bores. These are powerful waves that form at the head of an incoming tide and can travel at over 30 km per hour upstream. In Brazil, tidal bores are called pororocas, and they occur during the spring tide, in February and March each year. The approaching wave makes a loud roaring sound. The most powerful ones can sweep away animals, trees, and even houses. Despite the risks, some daredevil surfers have ridden the pororoca. The record ride for a pororoca surfer is 36 minutes.

Marajó

The largest island in the Amazon estuary is Marajó. It is the biggest freshwater island in the world, covering an area the size of Switzerland. It is only just above sea level and floods during the wet season. The island is made up of savannah, várzea forests, small farms and swamps. There is a large lake on the island which grows to 400 km² in the wet season. Farmers grow timber and açaí, a type of palm, and herd water buffalo.

Capybaras, which look like giant guinea pigs, live on Marajo. With their webbed feet, they are excellent swimmers and spend a lot of time in the water.

Damage from mining

The Amazon area is rich in minerals such as iron, copper and gold, which attract a wealth of mining people. Trees are cut down to provide fuel for iron-processing plants, which has added to local deforestation. Gold miners add mercury to the river to separate the gold from silt which poisons the fish. In the gold-mining areas of the Tapajós River, 90% of fish caught by rural villagers was contaminated with mercury. This chemical affects the nervous system and damages unborn babies.

JOURNEY'S END

Belém

Day 40-42, 22-24 February
Almeirim to Belém

I arrive at the port city of Belém, and I can't believe my journey has ended! Belém is a bustling, affluent city, but there is real, desperate poverty here too for people who were forced to leave the rainforest and now struggle to make a living. It makes me think back to all the changes I have seen on my journey down the river.

The city of Belém lies on the Pará River — the southern arm of the Amazon's mouth. Founded by the Portuguese in 1616, Belém is the gateway to the Amazon for people and goods arriving across the Atlantic. Cocoa, spices and sugar, as well as slaves, were shipped from here to Europe. Later, Belém became rich from the rubber trade. Today, the main products exported from here are nuts, pineapples, jute and hardwood timber.

The busy docks at Belém. The famous Ver-o-Peso Market in the background is one of the city's most famous landmarks.

betas
MARAJÓ
Almeirim
oidos
R. Pará
Belém
Santarém
ajós
Iriri

Amazon's end

The mouth of the Amazon includes both the Amazon itself and the Pará River to the south. The mouth as a whole is around 325 km wide and appears like an inland sea. Every year the river discharges over a million tonnes of silt into the ocean. Some of this silt has come all the way from the Andes Mountains, over 5,000 km away.

Future of the forest?

The rainforest and wildlife along the riverbank were an amazing sight, but it was sad to see that stretches of forest had been cleared to make way for cattle ranches. This has destroyed wildlife and the way of life of the Caboclos who live along the river. They were poor, but the forest gave them what they needed to survive. With the forest gone, they have no choice but to face poverty in the city. To save the Amazon we must reduce the amount of greenhouse gases such as carbon dioxide that we pump into the air from factories and vehicles. The rainforest locks up that gas, but with the forests gone, we lose that 'carbon store' – making climate change worse. Scientists fear that the Amazon will become so warm and dry by the end of this century that the river will shrink and the forest will die out.

Be smart, survive!

I can't stop climate change, but my journey has made me realise I need to do my bit when I get home!

1. I'll switch to energy-saving bulbs in my lights.
2. I'll switch off my computer and TV at the mains at night, rather than leave it on energy-guzzling standby.
3. I'll walk more or use trains and buses.

GLOSSARY

amphibian A cold-blooded class of animals that includes frogs, toads, newts and salamanders. They begin life as purely aquatic creatures with gills, and become lung-breathers as adults.

bacteria Single-celled microorganisms, some of which can cause disease.

bauxite A mineral from which aluminium is extracted.

blowgun A tube-shaped weapon through which an arrow or dart is propelled by force of breath.

camouflage An animal's colouring or shape that enables it to disguise itself by blending in with its surroundings; camouflage can also mean the disguising of people by painting or covering themselves so they blend in with their surroundings.

canopy The dense layer of leaves high above the ground in a forest.

clan A group of close-knit interrelated families.

contaminated Made impure by exposure to or addition of a poisonous or polluting substance.

deforestation Clearance of rainforests.

discharge The flowing out of a liquid or other substance into something else; for example, the discharge of a river into the sea.

ecosystem A community of interacting organisms and the physical environment around them.

estuary The tidal area near the mouth of a large river, where the tide meets the stream.

fishery A place where fish are caught or reared.

floodplain The flattish land on either side of a river, which often floods after heavy rain.

gorge A deep, narrow valley with steep sides.

hardwood Wood from a broad-leaved tree, as opposed to the softwood from conifers.

harpoon A spearlike missile.

igapó A flooded forest inundated with black water (water that has flowed through swamps).

indigenous Native to an area.

kayak A type of canoe made of a light frame with a watertight covering and a small opening at the top to sit in.

kindling Small sticks or twigs that burn easily, and are used for starting a fire.

loggers People who fell trees, legally or illegally.

machete A broad, heavy knife.

meander A looping bend on a river.

nutrients Nourishment.

orifice An opening in the body.

parasite An organism that lives in or on another organism (its host) and absorbs nutrients at the host's expense.

rainforest A dense forest, rich in plant and animal life, with consistently heavy rainfall, usually found in tropical areas.

rapids An area of white water, where a river crashes over rocks.

reserve A protected area.

secrete To discharge a substance from a cell or organ.

silt Fine sand or mud carried along by a river.

skiff A shallow, flat-bottomed open boat with a sharp bow and square stern.

spring tide A tide just after a new or full moon, when there is the greatest difference between high and low water.

tarpaulin Heavy-duty waterproof cloth.

tidal bore A wave formed at the leading edge of an incoming tide that travels up a river against the river's current.

toxic Poisonous.

tuber The fleshy underground stem or root of a plant.

upstream Towards the source of the river.

várzea A flooded forest inundated with white water (which is rich in mountain silt).

INDEX & FURTHER INFORMATION

Amazon rainforest 7, 8, 9, 10, 12-13, 17, 18, 19, 20, 21, 24, 28
Amazon River
  course 6
  current 6, 7
  estuary 26-27
  length 5
  tributaries 8
  volume 5
anaconda 16, 17
Andes Mountains 6, 18, 29
animals (see also names of individual animals) 9, 11, 12, 16, 17, 19, 20, 21, 26, 27, 29

birds 9, 12, 16, 17
blowguns and darts 9, 17
boats 10, 11, 24
Brazil 10, 12, 21, 22, 24, 26

caimans 5, 16, 17, 19
camouflage 17
capybaras 27
cattle ranches 29
cities 4, 6, 8, 11, 22, 24, 28, 29
climate 5
climate change 29
crafts 9

deforestation 13, 27, 29
dolphins 20, 25

farming 9, 13, 23, 27
festivals 8
fish 11, 13, 14-15, 16, 17, 19, 20, 23, 27
  arapaima 14
  bull sharks 25
  candiru 15
  electric eel 14
  piranhas 5, 15
  stingrays 25
  tambaqui 19
fishing 9, 10, 11, 13, 15
flooding 5, 18-19, 23, 24, 26, 27

harpoons 13, 19
hunting 9, 13, 15, 16, 17, 18, 23

logging 13

machetes 5, 13
manatee 21
minerals and mining 10, 27
monkeys 9, 12
mosquitoes 5, 13

nature reserves 21

palm trees 8
people 8-9, 10, 11, 17, 23, 29
  Bora people 8
  Caboclos 23, 29
  Yagua people 9
Peru 4, 6, 8
plants 7, 12, 20
poison dart frog 17

rubber 11, 22, 23, 28

seasons 5, 18, 20, 21, 23, 24, 26, 27
snakes (see also anaconda) 9, 17

tidal bores (pororoca) 26
tourism 11, 22, 24

Books

The Amazon (Journey along a River) by Jen Green (Wayland, 2009)
The Amazon (Rivers of the World) by Karen Gibson (Mitchell Lane, 2012)
The Amazon (River Adventure) by Paul Manning (Franklin Watts, 2012)

Websites

http://geography.howstuffworks.com/south-america/the-amazon-river.htm
http://www.bbc.co.uk/amazon/index.shtml
http://www.bbc.co.uk/learningzone/clips/exploring-the-amazon-river/7327.html
http://www.sciencekids.co.nz/sciencefacts/earth/amazonriver.html